SKILL BUILDER
GRAMMAR

LEVEL
2

T011632

PUFFIN BOOKS

An imprint of Penguin Random House

PUFFIN BOOKS

USA | Canada | UK | Ireland | Australia
New Zealand | India | South Africa | China

Puffin Books is part of the Penguin Random House group of companies
whose addresses can be found at global.penguinrandomhouse.com

Published by Penguin Random House India Pvt. Ltd
7th Floor, Infinity Tower C, DLF Cyber City,
Gurgaon 122 002, Haryana, India

First published in Puffin Books by Penguin Random House India 2021

Text, design and illustrations copyright © Quadrum Solutions Pvt. Ltd 2021
Series copyright © Penguin Random House India 2021

10 9 8 7 6 5 4 3 2 1

ISBN 9780143445043

Design and layout by Quadrum Solutions Pvt. Ltd
Printed at Aarvee Promotions, India

www.penguin.co.in

Dear Moms and Dads,

There's no better way to prepare your children for their future than to equip them with all the skills they need to grow into confident adults. The Skill Builder series has been created to hone subject skills as well as twenty-first century skills so that children develop not just academic skills but also life skills.

The books in the Skill Builder series focus on numerical, science and English language skills. Recognizing that children learn best while having fun, the books in this series have been created with a high 'fun' quotient. Each subject is dealt with across four levels, so you can choose the level that best suits your child's learning stage.

The Skill Builder: Grammar books have been created by academic experts who have devised a special chart to help you track the skills your child needs to master in order to understand and apply grammatical concepts.

It has been great creating this series with my highly charged Quadrum team—our academic experts, Krupa Shah and Naimisha Sanghavi, who spent hours crafting each page; Himani, who designed every page to be a visual treat; Gopi, who painstakingly laid out every word; Bishnupriya and Ruby, who read and reread every word; and Kunjli, who was the conscience of the entire series. And of course, the Puffin team—Sohini and Ashwitha—who added value at every step. When you have a great team, you're bound to have a great book.

I do hope you and your child enjoy the series as much as we have enjoyed creating it.

Sonia Mehta
PS: We'd love your feedback, so do write in to us at

funlearningbooks@quadrumltd.com

THE SKILL CHART

Here's a snapshot of the skills your child will acquire as they complete the activities:

- **Reading skills:** The ability to read and comprehend text with proficiency.
- **Writing skills:** The ability to form meaningful sentences and write with proficiency.
- **Speaking skills:** The ability to speak fluently and proficiently in the English language.
- **Punctuation skills:** The ability to use punctuation marks in the correct manner so as to form meaningful sentences.
- **Creative thinking skills:** The ability to view a problem creatively from different angles.
- **Decision-making skills:** The ability to choose between possible solutions to a problem through an intuitive or reasoned process, or both.
- **Critical thinking/problem-solving skills:** Rationalizing, analysing, evaluating and interpreting information to make informed judgements.

Page no.		Reading	Writing	Speaking	Punctuation	Creative thinking	Decision-making	Problem-solving/ Critical thinking
4	ADD AND REWRITE	☺	☺	☺				
5	FILL UP	☺	☺	☺				
6	HAPPY BIRTHDAY		☺		☺			☺
8	COLOUR COUNT			☺		☺	☺	
9	A, AN OR SOME?				☺	☺		
10	HOW MUCH OR HOW MANY?		☺	☺	☺	☺		☺
11	MAKE THEM COUNT		☺	☺			☺	
12	CIRCLE AWAY			☺				☺
13	PLURAL CROSSWORD	☺	☺			☺		☺
14	PLURAL SENTENCES		☺	☺		☺		☺
15	COLOUR THE PRONOUN		☺	☺			☺	
16	CIRCLED PRONOUNS	☺	☺				☺	☺
17	ADD THE PRONOUN		☺				☺	
18	PICTURE PRONOUNS		☺		☺	☺	☺	
19	CIRCLE THE VERB	☺						☺

20	THE WRONG VERB
21	FILL IN THE VERB
22	VERB SENTENCES
23	AWESOME ADJECTIVES
24	WRITE ALL ABOUT IT
26	CHOOSE RIGHT
27	PICTURE PREPOSITIONS
28	PICK THEM RIGHT
29	TIME TO CIRCLE
30	CHOOSE THE PREPOSITION
31	UNDERLINE RIGHT
32	FILL IN THE CONJUNCTIONS
33	MAKE SENTENCES
34	FILL IN THE BLANKS
35	FILL THE TABLE
36	WHAT'S THE RIGHT WORD?
37	FILL IT IN
38	PICTURE TALK
39	RIGHT OR NOT?
40	TENSE SENTENCES
42	COMPLETE THE TENSE
43	CIRCLE TIME
44	PICTURE-WORD RHYME
45	TIME TO PUNCTUATE
46	VISIT TO THE MARKET
47	PICK AND MAKE
49	FILL IN THE ADVERBS
50	COMPLETE THEM
51	ANSWER WITH ADVERBS
52	DETECTIVE DETERMINERS
53	COMPLETE THE SENTENCES
54	SHOE SENTENCES
55	CORRECT THEM ALL
56	SYNONYM SUNS
58	PICTURE ANTONYMS
59	PREFIX ANTONYMS

ADD AND REWRITE

Rewrite the following sentences using the articles a, an or the where required.

1. Sun shines brightly in sky.

   _____

2. I saw eagle yesterday.

   _____

3. Taj Mahal is in Agra.

   _____

4. It is good to eat apple day.

   _____

5. She wrote funny story.

   _____

FILL UP

Use a, an or the to complete the following sentences.

1   I got [   ] new bottle. [   ] bottle is green.

2   I need to buy [   ] umbrella and [   ] pair of boots.

3   [   ] Khans and [   ] Johnsons went out for dinner together.

4   There was [   ] octopus in [   ] sea.

5   I have [   ] brother and two sisters.

6   [   ] Great Wall of China is [   ] longest in [   ] world.

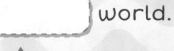

HAPPY BIRTHDAY

Look at the picture below. Write a paragraph describing the picture. Then, underline all the articles in your paragraph.

Colour all the pictures that show countable nouns.

Tip: Remember, a countable noun like *shirt* can be counted because there can be one or more of it (*one shirt, two shirts*). Uncountable nouns like *sunshine* or *water* cannot be counted.

A, AN OR SOME?

Fill in the blanks with a, an or some.

1. We bought [_____] butter and [_____] jam.

2. I bought [_____] hat.

3. I would like [_____] toothpaste.

4. Would you like [_____] tea or lemonade?

5. This is [_____] interesting book.

6. I ate [_____] biscuit and

   drank [_____] milk.

HOW MUCH OR HOW MANY?

For each picture below, frame a question that begins with 'how much' or 'how many'.

Tip: Remember, we use 'how many' for countable nouns and 'how much' for uncountable nouns.

1

2

3

4

5

MAKE THEM COUNT

Add a word or phrase to make these uncountable nouns countable. One has been done for you.

Tip: Use container or quantity words such as cup, kilo, box, etc.

1 cheese   **a slice of cheese** _____

2 rice _____

3 water _____

4 chocolate _____

5 jam _____

6 sunshine _____

7 rain _____

8 music _____

CIRCLE AWAY

Circle the correct plural form for each noun below.

leaves   leafs   leafes

car   cares   cars

radioes   radios   radioies

boy   boys   boyes

deeries   deeres   deer

hero   heroes   heros

PLURAL CROSSWORD

Complete the crossword using the plural forms of the nouns pictured.

13

PLURAL SENTENCES

Rewrite each sentence using the plural form of the word underlined in red.

Tip: Make sure you change any other words in the sentence that need to be changed as well!

1 There is a <u>hat</u> on the table.

_____

2 I have a red <u>apple</u>.

_____

3 There was a <u>bus</u> outside our school.

_____

4 I have a <u>bookshelf</u> in my room.

_____

COLOUR THE PRONOUN

Which noun does the underlined pronoun in each sentence refer to? Colour the correct box.

1   I saw Ms Sandra, but she didn't see me.

Ms Sandra	I

2   She ate a jam sandwich for breakfast.

the girl	jam sandwich

3   He ran very fast in the race.

the boy	race

4   Johnny called, he wanted to speak with you.

you	Johnny

5   They solved 20 maths problems every day.

the children	maths problems

6   I left my book in your room. Can you get it?

room	book

CIRCLED PRONOUNS

Underline the noun that is being referred to by
the circled pronoun in each sentence.

1   My friend lives in London. I don't see (her) often.

2   I am unable to open the jar so can you please
    open (it)?

3   Ron is in my class, but I don't know (him) well.

4   I see my friends every day and
    I always play with (them)

5   Tina called her mother to say (she) would be late.

6   Jiya does not have school today. Do you want to go
    to the beach with (her)?

ADD THE PRONOUN

Fill in the blanks with appropriate pronouns.

1   Mom and I went shopping. They gave [_____] a good discount.

2   The movie is very funny. I enjoy watching [_____].

3   Where is Paul? I didn't see [_____] in class today.

4   The Singhs are going to the mall. You can go with [_____].

5   Jessica is a friendly girl. I quite like [_____].

6   I can't find the butter. Did you finish [_____]?

PICTURE PRONOUNS

Write four sentences using nouns and pronouns to describe the picture below. Then, circle each noun and its matching pronoun in the same colour.

SCHOOL BUS

_____

_____

_____

_____

_____

_____

_____

_____

CIRCLE THE VERB

Circle all the different forms of the verb 'to be' in the sentences below.

1   I was going to get you a cookie.

2   You were late to class.

3   They will be going to the market in the evening.

4   We are going to watch a movie later.

5   I am very happy to see you.

6   I have been to Mei's house a couple of times.

7   She is the team's star performer.

THE WRONG VERB

Cross out (✗) the incorrect verb options in the sentences below.

1   They [was | were] travelling to town by bus.

2   I [is | am] going to bed early today.

3   They [have been | had been] waiting for you in the conference room for an hour now.

4   They [will | were] leave for school if you do not hurry up.

5   She [had been | will be] happy to see you.

6   My friend Hiram [has been | was] unwell yesterday.

7   [They was | They are] on time for the meeting.

FILL IN THE VERB

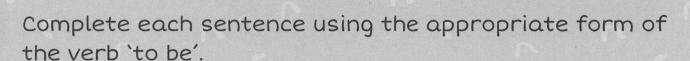

Complete each sentence using the appropriate form of the verb 'to be'.

1   We [   ] going to eat some ice cream.

2   It [   ] going to rain in the evening.

3   He [   ] finally able to open the window.

4   We [   ] coming to pick you up at five o'clock.

5   They [   ] making a lot of noise yesterday.

6   I [   ] going to buy a new dress for the party.

7   Maths [   ] a lot of fun.

Complete each sentence below using your own words.

1 He will be

_____

2 He had been

_____

3 I am

_____

4 They were

_____

5 She has been

_____

AWESOME ADJECTIVES

Fill in the blanks using appropriate adjectives.
Tip: Remember, an adjective is a word that helps to describe a noun.

1   The cat was playing with a [ ] ball.

2   The lion had [ ] teeth.

3   I saw a rabbit with [ ] ears.

4   He was riding a [ ] horse.

5   The mouse made a [ ] sound.

6   The dog found a [ ] bone.

7   The duck had [ ] feathers.

Describe these pictures in two sentences each. Be sure to use as many adjectives as you can.

CHOOSE RIGHT

Tick (✔) the adjective that is a better fit in each sentence below.

1   My mom is a [strong | delicious] woman.

2   Please pass me the [salty | silver] spoon.

3   The cookies were still [warm | wet] from the oven.

4   The [kind | sly] fox stole the bread.

5   Pritam played [melodious | hard] music.

6   The mangoes are very [beautiful | juicy].

7   I got a [new | sweet] dress.

PICTURE PREPOSITIONS

Describe the picture below in four or five sentences.
Be sure to use as many prepositions as you can.

Tip: Remember, a preposition tells us about the time when something happens, where something or someone is, or how something is done.

PICK THEM RIGHT

Fill in the blanks using appropriate prepositions from the box.

into   with   to   during   underneath   against

1   I had to go meet my teacher [   ] our lunch break.

2   Push the table [   ] the wall.

3   Give me the shirt [   ] the polka dots.

4   We went [   ] Grandma's house for lunch.

5   The parcel was kept [   ] the table.

6   He rammed the car [   ] the wall.

TIME TO CIRCLE

Circle the prepositions in the sentences below.

1 I want to sit by the window.

2 I will take a nap after lunch.

3 The car is parked in the garage.

4 We headed home from the airport.

5 Saima's party is on Saturday.

6 He likes mint ice cream with chocolate chips.

7 The cookie jar is in the cupboard.

29

CHOOSE THE PREPOSITION

Colour the preposition that is a better fit in each sentence below.

1 I put money   in | on   my piggy bank.

2 The dustbin is   on | under   the sink.

3 The books tumbled   off | into   the shelf.

4 The lion is sleeping   of | in   his den.

5 Klaus is going   on | up   the stairs.

6 The car went   through | off   the tunnel.

7 The horse jumped   under | over   the hurdle.

UNDERLINE RIGHT

Underline the conjunctions in the following sentences.
Tip: Remember, a conjunction (example: **but**) is a word that connects words, phrases or clauses in a sentence.

1   Would you like some tea or coffee?

2   How are Aamna and Jia doing?

3   I have cash, but I prefer paying by credit card.

4   Dad will stay at home tomorrow unless there is an important meeting.

5   I knew rain was forecast for today yet I forgot to take my umbrella.

6   I will leave early as I do not want to be stuck in traffic.

7   The lift was not working so I took the stairs.

FILL IN THE CONJUNCTIONS

Fill in the blanks using appropriate conjunctions.

1. I haven't finished the book [   ] I cannot lend it to you.

2. She missed her stop [   ] she had fallen asleep on the bus.

3. I took my umbrella [   ] gumboots.

4. She has a small car [   ] it has plenty of legroom.

5. Do you want to go to the beach [   ] the park?

6. I washed the dress [   ] the stain was still there.

7. I would like to buy some apples [   ] bananas.

MAKE SENTENCES

Look at the pictures below. Make sentences using these words as well as five different conjunctions.

FILL IN THE BLANKS

Fill in the blanks using appropriate conjunctions.

1   He likes going to the park [_____] he gets to play with his friends there.

2   I want a burger [_____] some fries.

3   I want some lemonade [_____] please don't add any ice.

4   They were tired [_____] they took a nap.

5   You should listen to him [_____] he is telling the truth.

6   Would you like the blue pen [_____] the black pen?

7   I can play the guitar [_____] the keyboard.

FILL THE TABLE

Fill in the table below with the correct comparative and superlative forms of the adjectives given.

One has been done for you.

Adjective	Comparative	Superlative
dark	darker	darkest
sad		
expensive		
short		
lazy		
pretty		
useful		
old		

WHAT'S THE RIGHT WORD?

Fill in the blanks with the comparative forms of the highlighted words.

1 The book I am reading is [_____] than yours. thick

2 The black dress is [_____] than the pink dress. elegant

3 Your bag is [_____] than Raj's. heavy

4 Suzie is [_____] than Rita. tall

5 Your house is [_____] than mine. big

6 The blue glass is [_____] than the green one. pretty

7 The horse is [_____] than the pig. fast

FILL IT IN

Fill in the blanks with the superlative forms of the highlighted words.

1   This mango is the [_____] of them all. `sweet`

2   I think the peacock is the [_____] bird. `beautiful`

3   Tariq is the [_____] boy in class. `smart`

4   Faye has the [_____] hair in the entire school. `long`

5   May is the [_____] month of the year. `warm`

6   It is the [_____] TV show now. `popular`

7   This sum is the [_____] . `difficult`

PICTURE TALK

Look at the pictures below and answer the questions that follow. Your answers must be complete sentences.

1   Which is the biggest animal?

_____

2   Between the hare and the horse, which is smaller?

_____

3   Which is the slowest of all?

_____

RIGHT OR NOT?

Read each sentence below. Draw a tick (✔) in the box if the sentence is correct or a cross (✗) if it is not.

1   I am liking to read books.

2   She is waiting at the bus stop for her friends.

3   She playing chess now.

4   The students were writing an essay yesterday.

5   Are you thinking about our vacation?

6   Be careful not be spilling the milk.

7   The radio is not work fine.

8   Fin will not be dancing tomorrow.

TENSE SENTENCES

Describe the pictures below in two sentences. You must use verbs in the present, past or future continuous tense in your sentences.

Tip: Add words such as *am, is, are, was, were,* and *will be* to the ing form of a verb to form in the continuous tense.

Picture 1:

_____

_____

_____

_____

_____

Picture 2:

_____

_____

_____

_____

_____

COMPLETE THE TENSE

Complete these sentences with the verbs in green written in the continuous tense form indicated.

1   I _____ not _____ at you. shout; past

2   Jack _____ _____ pasta
    for dinner. make; present

3   The birds _____ not _____ on the tree.
    sit; present

4   I _____ _____ _____ to the beach tomorrow.
    go; future

5   We _____ not _____ last week. travel; past

6   The boy _____ _____ his head.
    scratch; present

7   Rita _____ not _____ _____ milk tomorrow.
    drink; future

CIRCLE TIME

Circle the word in each row that rhymes with the word on the left.

Tip: Some words may be spelled differently but sound similar.

grow	blue	crow	cow	true
bear	hair	beat	year	flu
spark	speak	trap	bark	cry
sell	seal	sale	cell	tell
bank	bench	tank	book	trunk
fish	dish	pile	ship	wash
ring	feet	grim	pin	fling
take	slip	mile	flake	teak

PICTURE-WORD RHYME

Say the name of each image out loud. Then, read each sentence out loud and circle the word that rhymes with the image.

1    The orchestra played **loud** music.

2 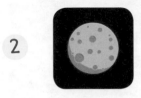   The cattle are expected to return **soon**.

3    The **clock** struck one. The mouse ran down.

4    There was a big green **frog**.

5    Daddy had a fierce **frown**.

6    We had lot of fun at the **fair**.

TIME TO PUNCTUATE

Rewrite these sentences by adding or removing the right punctuation marks.

1 john please send me the cake?

_____

2 I have! bought balloons streamers party Hats and confetti

_____

_____

3 Are you using a Glass bottle

_____

4 rita said this is virs winter jacket

_____

VISIT TO THE MARKET

Imagine you are going to the shops with your parents.

Make a list of the things you have to buy.

1 _____   5 _____

2 _____   6 _____

3 _____   7 _____

4 _____   8 _____

Describe your shopping trip in complete sentences.
Remember to use correct punctuation!

_____

_____

_____

_____

Write a dialogue you might have heard or participated in while you were out.

_____

_____

_____

_____

Frame two to three questions you might have asked a fruit or vegetable vendor.

_____

_____

_____

_____

PICK AND MAKE

Transform the adjectives in the box into adverbs. Then, complete each sentence using the right adverb.

> respectful   careful   eager   repeat
> effortless   greed   rare

1   The fox looked at the grapes _____.

2   Cross the road _____.

3   She painted _____.

4   It is important to argue _____ and not get angry.

5   It _____ rains in Rati's village.

6   The kids were waiting _____ for their grandparents to arrive.

7   Jay's parents reminded him _____ to complete his homework.

FILL IN THE ADVERBS

Complete this story using appropriate adverbs.

Tip: Think of different adverbs for each blank to avoid repeating an adverb.

It was a beautiful Sunday afternoon. Tia and Kia _____ stayed home on Sundays. That day, they decided to go down to the lake. They _____ enjoyed sitting and watching the birds. Kia got ready _____, but Tia was taking a long time. Kia _____ called out to Tia and asked her to hurry up. They _____ packed their picnic basket and left. The sun was shining _____ in the sky. They sat _____ by the lake and watched the birds _____. They _____ ate their sandwiches and drank their juices. They went home _____.

49

COMPLETE THEM

Complete these sentences in your own words. Make sure you use an adverb in each one. One has been done for you.

1   The king   **fought the war bravely.**

2   The birds   _____

3   The teacher   _____

4   An old lady   _____

5   The clouds   _____

6   Five snakes   _____

7   The little baby   _____

ANSWER WITH ADVERBS

Write answers to the questions below. You must use an adverb in each answer. One has been done for you.

1   How did Leena write her essay?

    Leena wrote her essay reluctantly.

2   When did Zeenab come home?

    _____

3   How did you eat the cake?

    _____

4   Where do you keep your books?

    _____

5   Do you eat out often?

    _____

DETECTIVE DETERMINERS

Read the story below and underline the determiners you find.

Tip: Remember, determiners come before nouns. They introduce nouns and tells us whether they are specific or general. There are four types: articles (a, an, the), demonstratives (this, that, these, those), possessives (my, your, his, her, your, their), quantifiers (some, few, little, many).

It was my friend Rahila's birthday. I went to her house for a party. It was a lovely pool party. The swimming pool was nicely decorated. She had invited many friends to her house. Everyone brought many presents for her. She thanked us all. She had three pet cats that played with us. Then it was time for us to cut the cake. There were seven candles on the cake. Those candles were sparkly. We also had some pizza, chips and fresh juice. Then it was time for us to go home. My parents came to pick me up. Rahila thanked me for coming. I had a great time.

COMPLETE THE SENTENCES

Write a determiner in the box to complete each sentence.

> her   their   our
> first   his   one   his

1   Ben has [   ] rabbit.

2   This is [   ] pencil.

3   I want [   ] bottle.

4   This is the [   ] book of its kind.

5   That is [   ] bag.

6   Where is [   ] car?

7   I am [   ] son.

SHOE SENTENCES

Look at this picture. Think of one sentence of each of the types indicated below. Write your sentences in the space given.

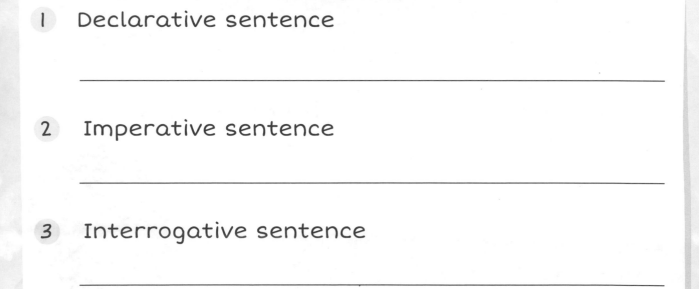

1 Declarative sentence

_____

2 Imperative sentence

_____

3 Interrogative sentence

_____

4 Exclamatory sentence

_____

CORRECT THEM ALL

Add the missing punctuation mark to each sentence. Then, write down what type of sentence each one is.

Tip: A sentence can be declarative, imperative, interrogative or exclamatory.

1 I have a green T-shirt

2 Help me

3 Go to your room now

4 I like crunchy apples

5 Did you see that car

6 I am very excited for the party

7 When are we leaving

8 Give me that spoon

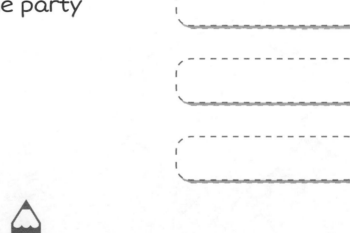

SYNONYM SUNS

Find a pair of words that have similar meanings and write them down inside one of the suns. Then, add a third word with a similar meaning to each sun.

speak

huge

wonderful

trash

knotty

marvellous

terrified

rubbish

gigantic

chat

frightened

hungry

starving

overjoyed

thrilled

drained

weary

difficult

PICTURE ANTONYMS

Write two describing words for each picture below. Then, write their opposites. One has been done for you.

heavy	X	light
long	X	

	X	
	X	

	X	
	X	

	X	
	X	

PREFIX ANTONYMS

Can you add the right prefix to each word below to turn it into its opposite?

Tip: Sometimes, a word can be turned into its opposite by adding *im, un, il, mis, in* or *dis* to the beginning of the word.

1   Jack [   ] understood Mona.

2   The water was [   ] pure.

3   Lakyle has not given us any reason to [   ] trust him.

4   Your handwriting is [   ] legible.

5   The oil had an [   ] pleasant smell.

6   Your answer is [   ] correct.

ANSWERS

page 4 ADD AND REWRITE

1. The sun shines brightly in the sky. 2. I saw an eagle yesterday. 3. The Taj Mahal is in Agra. 4. It is good to eat an apple a day. 5. She wrote a funny story.

page 5 FILL UP

1. a, The; 2. an, a; 3. The, the; 4. an, the; 5. a; 6. The, the, the

pages 6–7 HAPPY BIRTHDAY

Answers will vary.

page 8 COLOUR COUNT

page 9 A, AN OR SOME?

1. some, some; 2. a; 3. some; 4. some; 5. an; 6. a, some

page 10 HOW MUCH OR HOW MANY?

1. How much paint is in the can? OR How many cans of paint are there?

2. How many books are there?

3. How much juice is in the glass? OR How many glasses of juice are there?

4. How many bananas are there in the basket? OR How many baskets of bananas are there?

5. How much money is in the sack? OR How many coins are in the sack? OR How many sacks of coins are there?

page 11 MAKE THEM COUNT

Some possible answers: 2. a grain of rice; 3. a bottle of water; 4. a bar of chocolate; 5. a jar of jam; 6. a ray of sunshine; 7. a drop of rain; 8. a piece of music OR a note of music

page 12 CIRCLE AWAY

Words to be circled: leaves, cars, radios, boys, deer, heroes

page 13 PLURAL CROSSWORD

page 14 PLURAL SENTENCES

1. There are hats on the table. 2. I have some red apples. 3. There were buses outside our school. 4. I have bookshelves in my room.

page 15 COLOUR THE PRONOUN

1. I saw Ms Sandra, but <u>she</u> didn't see me. — Ms Sandra | I

2. <u>She</u> ate a jam sandwich for breakfast. — the girl | jam sandwich

3. <u>He</u> ran very fast in the race. — the boy | race

4. Johnny called, <u>he</u> wanted to speak with you. — you | Johnny

5. <u>They</u> solved 20 maths problems every day. — the children | maths problems

6. I left my book in your room. Can you get <u>it</u>? — room | book

page 16 CIRCLED PRONOUNS

1. my friend; 2. jar; 3. Ron; 4. my friends; 5. Tina; 6. Jiya

page 17 ADD THE PRONOUN

1. us; 2. it; 3. him; 4. them; 5. her; 6. it

page 18 PICTURE PRONOUNS

Answers will vary.

page 19 CIRCLE THE VERB

Words to be circled: 1. was; 2. were; 3. will be; 4. are; 5. am; 6. have been; 7. is

page 20 THE WRONG VERB

Boxes to be crossed out: 1. was; 2. is; 3. had been; 4. were; 5. had been; 6. has been; 7. They was

page 21 FILL IN THE VERB

1. are; 2. is; 3. was; 4. are, 5. were; 6. am; 7. is

page 22 VERB SENTENCES

Answers will vary.

page 23 AWESOME ADJECTIVES

Answers will vary.

pages 24–25 WRITE ALL ABOUT IT

Answers will vary.

page 26 CHOOSE RIGHT

1. strong; 2. silver; 3. warm; 4. sly; 5. melodious; 6. juicy; 7. new

page 27 PICTURE PREPOSITIONS

Answers will vary.

page 28 PICK THEM RIGHT

1. during; 2. against; 3. with; 4. to; 5. underneath; 6. into

page 29 TIME TO CIRCLE

Words to be circled: 1. by; 2. after; 3. in; 4. from; 5. on; 6. with; 7. in

page 30 CHOOSE THE PREPOSITION

1. in; 2. under; 3. off; 4. in; 5. up; 6. through; 7. over

page 31 UNDERLINE RIGHT

Words to be underlined: 1. or; 2. and; 3. but; 4. unless; 5. yet; 6. as; 7. so

page 32 FILL IN THE CONJUNCTIONS

1. so; 2. as; 3. and; 4. yet OR but; 5. or; 6. but OR yet; 7. and

page 33 MAKE SENTENCES

Answers will vary.

page 34 FILL IN THE BLANKS

1. as; 2. and; 3. but; 4. so; 5. because; 6. or; 7. and

page 35 FILL THE TABLE

Adjective	Comparative	Superlative
dark	darker	darkest
sad	sadder	saddest
expensive	more expensive	most expensive
short	shorter	shortest
lazy	lazier	laziest
pretty	prettier	prettiest
useful	more useful	most useful
old	older	oldest

page 36 WHAT'S THE RIGHT WORD?

1. thicker; 2. more elegant; 3. heavier; 4. taller; 5. bigger; 6. prettier; 7. faster

page 37 FILL IT IN

1. sweetest; 2. most beautiful; 3. smartest; 4. longest; 5. warmest; 6. most popular; 7. most difficult

page 38 PICTURE TALK

1 The elephant is the biggest animal.

2 The hare is smaller than the horse.

3 The snail is the slowest of all.

page 39 RIGHT OR NOT?

Sentences to be ticked: 2, 4, 5, 8; Sentences to be marked with a cross: 1, 3, 6, 7

pages 40–41 TENSE SENTENCES

Answers will vary.

page 42 COMPLETE THE TENSE

1. was, shouting; 2. is making; 3. are, sitting; 4. will be going; 5. were, travelling; 6. is scratching; 7. will, be drinking

page 43 CIRCLE TIME

Words to be circled: crow, hair, bark, tell, tank, dish, fling, flake

page 44 PICTURE-WORD RHYME

1. loud; 2. soon; 3. clock; 4. frog; 5. frown; 6. fun

page 45 TIME TO PUNCTUATE

1. john please send me the cake?

   John, please send me the cake.

2. I have! bought balloons streamers party Hats and confetti

   I have bought balloons, streamers, party hats

   and confetti.

3. Are you using a Glass bottle

   Are you using a glass bottle?

4. rita said this is virs winter jacket

   Rita said, 'This is Vir's winter jacket.'

pages 46–47 VISIT TO THE MARKET
Answers will vary.

page 48 PICK AND MAKE
1. greedily; 2. carefully; 3. effortlessly; 4. respectfully; 5. rarely; 6. eagerly; 7. repeatedly

page 49 FILL IN THE ADVERBS
Some possible answers: usually, really, quickly, finally, hurriedly, brightly, quietly, happily, merrily, early

page 50 COMPLETE THEM
Answers will vary.

page 51 ANSWER WITH ADVERBS
Answers will vary.

page 52 DETECTIVE DETERMINERS

It was my friend Rahila's birthday. I went to her house for the party. It was a lovely pool party. The swimming pool was nicely decorated.

She had invited many friends to her house. Everyone brought many presents for her. She thanked us all. She had three pet cats that played with us. Then it was time for us to cut the cake. There were seven candles on the cake. Those candles were sparkly. We also had some pizza, chips and fresh juice. Then it was time for us to go home. My parents came to pick me up. Rahila thanked me for coming. I had a great time.

page 53 COMPLETE THE SENTENCES
1. one; 2. her; 3. his; 4. first; 5. my; 6. our; 7. their

page 54 SHOE SENTENCES
Answers will vary.

page 55 CORRECT THEM ALL

1. I have a green T-shirt.   declarative

2. Help me!   exclamatory

3. Go to your room now.   imperative

4. I like crunchy apples.   declarative

5. Did you see that car?   interrogative

6. I am very excited for the party!   exclamatory

7. When are we leaving?   interrogative

8. Give me that spoon.   imperative

pages 56–57 SYNONYM SUNS
Some possible answers:

huge	trash	hungry
gigantic	rubbish	starving
enormous	garbage	famished

frightened	marvellous	chat
terrified	wonderful	speak
horrified	spectacular	converse

knotty	drained	overjoyed
difficult	weary	thrilled
complicated	exhausted	ecstatic

page 58 PICTURE ANTONYMS
Some possible answers:
heavy x light, long x short; cold x hot, sweet x sour; dirty x clean, wet x dry; many x few, empty x full

page 59 PREFIX ANTONYMS
1. misunderstood; 2. impure; 3. distrust; 4. illegible; 5. unpleasant; 6. incorrect